KING GEORG

A Life from Beginning to End

Copyright © 2017 by Hourly History

Table of Contents

Introduction

For members of the royal family, particularly those who will inherit the throne, it is imperative that they are married and produce at least two children. One child is to succeed a title, such as Your Royal Highness, and one child is to guarantee the family line should anything happen to the first. In British culture, this imperative is jokingly known as "an heir and a spare." King George VI, named Albert at birth and known as such until he succeeded the throne, was born on the 14th of December 1895, the second son of Prince George (later King George V) and his wife, Mary. Albert was "the spare," and his experience of growing up in his older, more charming and accomplished brother's shadow affected his life to such an extent that he ultimately became the man more fit to rule.

Characterized by his stammer, a verbal quirk that made him famous among contemporary audiences thanks to the 2006 film *The King's Speech*, the young Albert was a less social man than his older brother, David. Both David and Albert served in the Royal Navy and saw active service during the First World War, but it was Albert who stayed close to his father, King George V, supporting him in his many often tedious duties as King, while David, the Duke of York, lived the fast lifestyle of a socialite.

The story of David's short time on the throne as King Edward VIII is legendary. Unwilling to change his lifestyle to fulfill the serious duties that came with the title of King of the United Kingdom and the Dominions of the British Empire and Emperor of India, Edward VIII's unsuitability for the demands of kingship was remarked upon before King George V had even died. Edward VIII's relationship with, and subsequent marriage to, a twice-divorced American woman of "common" blood, coupled with his pro-German sympathies, caused the royal family and Great Britain's political body to close ranks. In order to marry the woman he loved, the King was forced to abdicate.

George VI never wanted the throne of Great Britain, but once he had it, he committed himself fully to the duty of serving his public. With his extensive military knowledge, sensible nature, and skill in the art of diplomacy, George VI came to the throne just in time to lead the nation through the devastating Second World War. The Royal Family's conduct during the war and the King's close relationship with his formidable Prime Minister, Winston Churchill, helped the nation to fall in love with the Windsors, but the war had taken its toll on the King's health. A very heavy smoker from the age of eighteen and prone to anxiety and sleeplessness, the King's health began to fail before he reached the age of 55.

The Second World War changed the world and had a dramatic effect on Great Britain. At home, the political landscape shifted dramatically, and in the post-war years, the Labour party took control of the country, revolutionizing the welfare system and improving the lives of the working class. Great Britain's role abroad changed too as India gained its independence, the British Empire collapsed, and the Commonwealth was formed. The King lived long enough to see his eldest daughter Princess Elizabeth marry, have two children, and take on a number of royal responsibilities at home and abroad. When George

VI died on the 6th of February 1952 and Elizabeth succeeded to the throne, she did so with a sense of duty and honor that mirrored that of her father.

Chapter One

Early Years

"I don't dislike babies, though I think very young ones rather disgusting."

—Queen Victoria

When Albert was born, his great-grandmother, seventy-six-year-old Victoria, Queen of Great Britain and Ireland and Empress of India, was still on the throne. The young Prince's date of birth, 14th of December 1895, fell on a day deemed painfully inauspicious by Queen Victoria as it was the date of the death of her husband Prince Albert and her daughter Princess Alice of Hesse. Albert was the second son of Prince George, Duke of York (later King George V) and Mary, Duchess of York (Later Queen Mary).

The Duke of York, although thrilled to have been blessed with a second son, was fearful of how his formidable mother might react to news of Albert's birth. The family rallied and tried to lift Victoria out of her habitual annual mourning by suggesting that Albert's birth might be seen as a gift from God, sent to make Victoria happy on the saddest day of the year. The Duke of York's insistence that Albert should be named after his great-grandfather also went some way in gaining Victoria's favor. Albert was named Prince Albert Frederick Arthur

George of York and baptized at St Mary Magdalene's Church near Sandringham at three months old.

At his birth, Prince Albert was fourth in line to the throne of Great Britain and Ireland after his grandfather, father, and older brother David. Thanks to the work of Queen Victoria, referred to during the later years of her reign as the "grandmother of Europe," young princes David and Albert were members of a huge and far-reaching royal family whose influence stretched across Europe and Russia. By the time Prince Albert was in his last years as King, there were twenty reigning monarchs in continental Europe, and he was related to all of them by bonds of blood or marriage. George VI viewed his position in this collective royal family as a profession and even referred to the royal family as the "family firm."

After the birth of Prince Albert, the Duchess of York gave birth to Princess Mary in 1897, Prince Henry in 1900, Prince George in 1902, and Prince John in 1905. Although Sandringham itself was a huge building, the young family lived at York Cottage, a small house on the grounds. The children were raised by hired nannies with little day-to-day influence from their mother and father and existed almost entirely in two small rooms, a "day nursery" and "night nursery." Ordinarily, the children would spend just one hour a day with their parents, usually at tea-time, and Prince Albert grew up feeling disconnected from his father, who spent little time at home and was known for his strictness and explosive temper.

Prince George had been sent away to join the Navy while still an adolescent and had learned discipline and subordination the hard way aboard HMS Britannia. Albert and his siblings were treated as young navy officers by their father, who demanded that they keep to their quarters as much as possible and when in the presence of adults behave as though they were adults themselves. Perhaps due in part to the stress of this incredibly strict upbringing and neglect suffered at the hands of nannies, something all too common in upper-class households at the time, Albert was in poor health as a child. Albert had stomach problems, knock knees and a stammer that grew worse the older he got. Despite being left-handed, he was forced to write with his right hand and punished for his bad handwriting skills.

On the 22nd of January 1901, Queen Victoria died and Albert's grandfather, the Prince of Wales, succeeded to the throne of Great Britain and Ireland. On the 9th of August 1902, almost eighteen months later, King Edward VII and Queen Alexandra were crowned at a coronation ceremony in Westminster Abbey, attended by a sea of crowned heads. The lives of David and Albert changed abruptly at this point. Now that their father, George, was created the Prince of Wales, he was forced to occupy a more public role in the royal family and left on long processions overseas, leaving his children to the care of the delighted King and Queen, who spoiled the children and let them run riot around their opulent palaces. Soon, though, life settled down again, the two boys' education started in earnest with the appointment of an uninspiring tutor, Mr. Hansell.

Albert became increasingly shy; his stammer worsened, and he was forced to endure painful splints in an attempt to cure him of his knock knees. The educational curriculum prepared by Mr. Hansell, a former schoolmaster, was unfamiliar and challenging for the two boys, and they endured their schooldays going from tutor to tutor with little success. In January 1909, aged just thirteen, Prince Albert left York House to join the Royal Naval College in Osborne, two years after David had made the same difficult journey.

Chapter Two

Prince Albert in the Navy

"Si vis pacem, para bellum/ If you wish for peace, prepare for war."

—Royal Navy motto

George's desire that his sons be treated the same as any other naval cadet were hard to maintain, not least because Osborne, the location of the Royal Naval College, was the very place Queen Victoria had died eight years previously. King Edward VII hated the building and refused to take it on, instead giving it to the nation to be used as a soldier's convalescence home and naval college. Albert and his peers were housed in the stable block where they endured Spartan accommodations.

Albert was small for his age and was mercilessly bullied by the other cadets. After the second year of his studies, Albert finished last in his class, scoring 68th out of 68 cadets. Nonetheless, he went on to the second stage of his naval education at the Dartmouth Royal Naval College where both Princes were struck down with measles and mumps, a disease that can lead to sterility in adolescent and adult men. While Albert seems to have avoided further complications, it's possible that this disease left David, currently second in line to the English throne, sterile.

In May 1910, soon after the young princes' illness, their grandfather King Edward VII died. Having ruled for just nine years, Edward VII was succeeded by George, who became King George V. Prince David, Albert's older brother, was created Prince of Wales, and Albert moved up another position to become, aged just fourteen, second in line to the throne. Now that his father was King, Albert's life was transformed. The family inherited the royal palaces and moved into Buckingham Palace in London but also spent a great deal of time at Windsor, where George reclaimed his grandmother's simple, frugal domestic life, prompting some to remark that the monarchy had regressed back to Victorian times. The young Princes found themselves under more scrutiny than ever before in the eyes of the public, the royal court, parliament and the extended royal family they were surrounded by at Windsor and Buckingham Palace. Albert had always nursed an inferiority complex when it came to his older, healthier, more loquacious brother, but now that David was the Prince of Wales, he found himself utterly eclipsed.

In the winter of 1911, Albert returned to Dartmouth College and in May 1912 accompanied his father on the royal yacht Victoria & Albert at the review of the naval fleet. It was on this occasion that Albert first experienced an underwater dive in a submarine and met Winston Churchill, then First Lord of the Admiralty. In early 1913 Albert was sent to serve aboard the HMS Cumberland, a cruiser that would be his home for the duration of a six-month training voyage. This cruise entailed a round trip of the British Empire's lands in the Western Atlantic, the West Indies, and Canada. The attention the King's son aroused with locals at each port of call caused Albert incredible embarrassment, and he was desperate to blend in with the other cadets. In September of the same year, Albert received his first naval commission as a qualified midshipman aboard the battleship HMS Collingwood.

Albert spent three months aboard the Collingwood, taking part in maneuvers in the Mediterranean. During this time he was taken by Admiral Sir Berkeley Milne to stay with Lord Kitchener, his father's friend, in Cairo, Egypt, where he was presented to the Khedive and taken to see the pyramids. During his time on the Collingwood, Albert was referred to as "Johnson," a nickname devised to keep his identity secret. Albert's superior officers endeavored to treat the King's son exactly the same as the other junior midshipmen, but in reality, this was impossible, as Albert was constantly in the public eye, an experience he never became comfortable with.

Chapter Three

The Great War

"I was so glad old Bertie was in the fight, it will buck him up a lot."

— The Prince of Wales on Prince Albert

Albert was aboard the Collingwood on the 28th of June, 1914, when Archduke Franz Ferdinand and his wife were assassinated in Sarajevo, effectively starting the First World War. The seriousness of this event was not immediately felt by those in power in Great Britain. Neither the government, royal family, nation, nor least of all Albert, who didn't even log the event in his diary, realized that this assassination would trigger one of the deadliest conflicts in history, a war that would eventually culminate in the deaths of over 38 million people.

In Great Britain, the Royal Navy mobilized for war on the 15th of July 1914 and a grand review of the entire fleet was held, led by First Admiral Winston Churchill. Austria declared war on Serbia, and Albert was sent aboard the Collingwood to the Scapa Flow to guard the northern entrance to the North Sea. Albert's wartime service had lasted just three weeks before he was diagnosed with appendicitis and taken to Aberdeen University Hospital for surgery. Young men who stayed home wearing civilian clothes while their peers took up arms and fought for their country were the subject of much stigma at this time and, keen to avoid being labeled a coward, Albert boarded the Collingwood once again in February 1915. Again he was struck down with gastric problems and, suffering from a misdiagnosed stomach ulcer, spent painful months trying to recuperate back on land. During this time at home with his father, King George V, Albert learned a great deal about the business of kingship and absorbed many important lessons about international politics. Albert turned twenty-one on the 14th of December 1916, an occasion marked by his receiving the Order of the Garter.

In 1917 King George V attempted to rid the royal family of its undeniably strong ties to Germany by changing the family name. The royal family was to no longer use the name Saxe-Coburg-Gotha, the title of Queen Victoria's husband Prince Albert, and took on the name Windsor instead. Albert finally saw the naval combat he desired at the Battle of Jutland that took place between the 31st of May and the 1st of June and was the most significant engagement between the German and British navies of the war. Albert served as a turret officer during the conflict that turned out to be an indecisive battle, with both sides suffering great losses and both claiming victory. The young prince escaped injury and, as the only deaths he had witnessed had been glimpsed from his turret through mist and smoke, he was able to retain his boyish idea of war as being glorious and exciting.

Eventually, in November 1917, Albert was correctly diagnosed with a duodenal ulcer and given an operation to treat it. The operation was a success; finally, the bouts of extreme pain, fatigue, and mental wretchedness that come with a stomach ulcer were over. Of his four years as a serving naval officer, Albert had been at sea for just twenty-two months. Not content to return to civilian life with war on the continent still raging, Albert joined the Royal Naval Air Service in February 1918, the last year of the war. After spending two months as an Officer in Charge of Boys aboard HMS Daedalus at Cranwell in Lincolnshire, Albert transferred to the newly created Royal Air Force and was given the rank of captain.

The Prince was unhappy at Cranwell. To him, the newly formed air force was disorganized, with Navy and Army protocol battling it out on a daily basis. Albert also failed to achieve the same tight social circle he had enjoyed aboard the HMS Collingwood and eventually obtained his release from Cranwell. In August 1918 he served with the 5 Cadet wing at the RAF headquarter at St Leonards-on-Sea, where he became head of the squadron. Desperate to see action in France, Albert was flown across the channel to Autigny in the final weeks of the war where he served at the Independent Air Force Headquarters. The bold German military initiative of 1918 had failed, and since then German troops had been in retreat. On the 11th of November 1918 at 11 o'clock guns fell silent on the Western Front and the war was finally over. Albert stayed on the continent for a further two months, and on 31 July 1919 became certified as a fully qualified pilot, the first member of the royal family ever to do so.

Chapter Four

Lady Elizabeth Bowes-Lyon

"...he is a man who will be made or marred by his wife."

— Cecilia Countess of Strathmore on King George VI

After the war, it was decided that Albert should have a university education and he was sent, along with his younger brother Prince Henry, to study at Trinity College, Cambridge for one year. The only subjects Albert studied were history, economics, and civics and he left Cambridge with no more friends than he had when joined, his only real companion being his cousin Lord Louis Mountbatten. Longing for the family life he had left behind at Sandringham and some semblance of the discipline and ritual he had become accustomed to as part of the Navy, Albert joined the Brotherhood of Freemasons in 1919. Known as the "craft," freemasonry has levels of membership and Albert made a rapid ascent up the masonic ladder.

While the Prince of Wales was constantly on tour, visiting the imperial nations of the British Empire and becoming the public face of the British Royal Family, Albert carried out duties on the home front. In June 1920, King George created Albert the Duke of York, and he represented his father in Great Britain, making extensive tours of industrial locations, such as mines, factories, and shipyards. Eventually, the Prince became President of the Industrial Welfare Society and gained the nickname "the foreman" within his family due to his dedication to improving industry and interest in technical processes. Albert was also sent as a representative of the royal family to the coronation of Marie and Ferdinand, the King and Queen of Greater Romania, an area of land that included Transylvania but had been given to Romania following the war.

Now aged twenty-four, Albert had a little more freedom than he enjoyed as a small boy living in York House and presided over by a nanny - but only a little. The King kept a strict eye on both of his sons and was extremely anxious about either of them getting involved with "bad women" and causing a scandal, as he had witnessed numerous male members of his family do since childhood. Court life, which under the aging King George V and Queen Mary seemed to have changed little from Queen Victoria's time, was dull for the young Princes, and each tried to loosen the King's grip on their lives. David had it fairly easy as although he was always in the public eye he spent the majority of his time abroad, touring the Empire. Albert, by comparison, was a stay at home son. When Princess Mary was married in February 1922 to Viscount Lascelles, Albert became the only occupant of the section of Buckingham Palace designated for "the children." It was time for Albert to find a wife.

Albert had experienced brief and barely notable flings with a number of women at this time, among them dancer

Phyllis Monkman, Lady Maureen Cane-Tempest-Stewart, and the married socialite Sheila, Lady Loughborough. Then, on the 10th of June 1920, at a Derby Night ball at Buckingham Palace, Albert met nineteen-year-old Lady Elizabeth Bowes-Lyon. Elizabeth was the daughter of the Earl and Countess of Strathmore and Kinghorne and had met Albert fourteen years before. She was five at the time and he was ten. Albert later said that he fell in love with Elizabeth that night and became determined to marry her. 5 foot 4 inches in height with a beautiful complexion and wearing an old-fashioned dress with an unflattering haircut, Elizabeth caught Albert's eye due in part to her difference from the chain-smoking and cocktail dress-wearing women he was frequently introduced to. Having been catapulted into an adult world at the outbreak of war, at which time she was only fourteen, Elizabeth's debut had been postponed until 1920, and she soon found herself at the center of a social whirlwind where Albert was not her only admirer.

After a protracted courtship, during which Elizabeth rejected Albert's proposal twice, the pair were engaged to be married. Although undeniably aristocratic with a family tree stretching back to the Middle Ages, Elizabeth was not of royal birth, and Albert's decision to marry her was seen by many as a welcome attempt to modernize the royal family. Elizabeth did not take the decision to marry into the royal family lightly and took almost three years to make up her mind finally. She had seen enough of life at the Court to understand that her marriage to Albert would be under constant observation and her performance, as a wife and, in time, a mother would always be subject to the worst kind of public scrutiny.

However, on the 26th of April 1923, Elizabeth and Albert were married in Westminster Abbey, the first wedding of a royal prince in over 500 years. Compared to the royal weddings that had preceded it, the wedding of Albert and Elizabeth was a fairly simple and practical affair, although it did feature a nine-foot wedding cake and gifts of priceless jewels. The wedding organizers took advantage of the latest technology and filmed the proceedings, although the footage was never shown as the Abbey Chapter vetoed the idea, fearing subjects might watch the ceremony in public houses.

"The Yorks," as they were now to be known, spent their honeymoon at Polesden Lacey in Surrey before retiring to their married home of White Lodge in Richmond Park, a home chosen for them by the King and Queen. "Retired" is perhaps an apt word, as the lifestyle of the young couple was closer to that of the King and Queen than their peers, such as Albert's brother, the Prince of Wales. While the Prince of Wales was firmly established at the heart of the fast and fashionable London set who danced until dawn at London's most glamorous nightclubs and holidayed in the most happening places abroad, the Yorks maintained a more traditional lifestyle and only went abroad in the line of duty.

Duty saw the Yorks touring Kenya, Uganda, and the Sudan between December 1924 and April 1925. Both husband and wife had been raised to enjoy hunting and indulged themselves in big game hunting expeditions during this tour. Four years into the Yorks' married life,

Elizabeth gave birth to their first child, Princess Elizabeth, on the 21st of April 1926 by caesarean section. Albert was thrilled and gushed over the little princess in letters to her parents. Thankfully no negative comments were made about the couple's firstborn being a girl; after all, no one thought that the child would ever succeed to the throne.

Elizabeth's high society upbringing and naturally cheerful personality were a godsend to Albert, who had always dreaded carrying out his public duties. With gentle encouragement and an ability to attract attention away from Albert and onto herself, Elizabeth managed to avert what we would now call PR disasters at official functions. However, Elizabeth could not deflect public attention from the difficulty Albert encountered when giving speeches. At the closing of the British Empire Exhibition at Wembley Stadium on the 31st of October 1925, Albert was required to give a speech in the absence of the Prince of Wales who had left on a tour of Southern Africa. The speech was an awful ordeal for Albert, whose debilitating stammer made it near impossible at times for him to express himself. The King and Queen despaired, and most of the country agreed that Albert was unfit to represent Great Britain in public.

This speech marked a low point in Albert's life, but there was a silver lining to the experience; standing in the crowd that day was none other than Lionel Logue, an Australian speech therapist who was convinced that he could cure Albert. An appointment was arranged between the Duke and Mr. Logue at his Harley Street consulting room for the 19th of October 1926. Albert met with Lionel at his consulting rooms every week for a number of months and noticed an instant improvement in his speech. In

January 1927 Albert embarked on his first major imperial tour, representing both his father the King and Great Britain itself, in Australia and New Zealand.

With the Duchess at his side and Logue's teachings and daily exercises at the forefront of his mind, Albert was able to give the necessary speeches without hesitation. At the opening ceremony of the new Parliament House in Canberra, Australia, Albert astounded everyone with his delivery. Albert's relationship with his father had long been a difficult one, with the King prone to belittling Albert and criticizing his every move. Following Albert's performance in Australia and New Zealand, the King's treatment of Albert warmed, and he held him in higher esteem than ever before, a shift that served to make the King's opinion of his other son, David, even worse.

Chapter Five

The Reign and Abdication
of King Edward VIII

"After I am dead the boy will ruin himself in twelve months."

—King George V on the Prince of Wales

The relationship between King George V and the Prince of Wales was almost completely devoid of affection. As George aged and became more fragile and prone to health problems he made it clear that he did not think that David was worthy of the throne, saying, "I pray to God that my eldest son will never marry and that nothing will come between Bertie and Lillibet and the throne." David had a reputation for fast living and his fondness for nightclubs, heavy drinking, and sexual promiscuity gave senior members of the British government, as well as members of his own royal entourage, ammunition to accuse him of being completely unsuitable for kingship. In an interview with the then Prime Minister Stanley Baldwin, David's Private Secretary Alan Lascelles said, "the Heir Apparent, in his unbridled pursuit of wine and women, and whatever selfish whim occupied him at that moment, was rapidly going to the devil..." and that he "couldn't help thinking that the best thing that could happen to him, and the country, would be for him to break his neck."

Between late November and early December 1927, while the Prince of Wales was on a safari holiday in Kenya, King George V became gravely ill with a bronchial infection that soon turned into an infection of the blood. Unwilling to cut his holiday short, the Prince of Wales' position as the King's deputy in the event of illness was filled by Albert, who became a temporary member of the Council of State. The King began to regain his health, but his recovery was slow and hampered by the fact that he continued to smoke and recommenced his public duties while recovering.

The King's brush with death seemed to bring about a reconciliation of sorts between David and him, and both brothers were able to enjoy their father's company for a peaceful few months. By now the Yorks were comfortably settled in their home at 145 Picadilly, London, a handsome if fairly modest home for a future King. In 1931 the family was gifted the Royal Lodge in Windsor Great Park by the King and Queen and spent a number of years renovating it as Albert indulged his passion for gardening. On the 21st of August 1930, Elizabeth gave birth to Princess Margaret Rose and the royal family was complete.

With Albert so thoroughly happy and settled in his home life, it became a matter of serious urgency that a suitable wife be found for David. Over his years of bachelordom, the Prince of Wales had demonstrated a marked preference for married women, a habit that his father abhorred but perhaps suited David as a way of ensuring that a marriage between him and his conquests would be out of the question. Before Wallis Simpson entered David's life, he spent a great deal of time with a woman named Freda Dudley Ward, later turning his attentions to Thelma Morgan Furness, a starlet of American high society. Thelma was a hit with the Yorks who attended many parties at the Fort, David's preferred abode, but once Wallis Simpson entered his life, the Yorks were conspicuous in their absence.

The royal family took an almost instant dislike to Wallis, whom they labeled common, a woman of low birth, already divorced with no fortune, whose interest in the royals was purely mercenary. What's more, she was American. The Prince of Wales fell deeply in love with Wallis in the summer of 1934, to the horror of his parents and Prince Albert. When news of the affair hit the press, middle-class society across the empire reacted with great offense, to which the Prince of Wales countered that his private life was his own affair. The Prince of Wales further antagonized the royal family by inviting Mrs. Simpson and her husband to important events such as the State Ball. It became clear to all that the Prince of Wales and Wallis Simpson were engaged in an affair and it was said that Wallis was the dominant force in the relationship, "bewitching" the Prince to do her bidding.

King George V died on the 20th of January 1936, aged seventy. A bulletin issued on the evening of his death stated, "The King's life is moving peacefully towards its close." The King's doctor, Lord Dawson of Penn, saw to it that George was given a sedative, followed by two lethal injections of morphine and cocaine in order to hasten his death. The reasoning given for the administering of euthanasia, an act carried out without the consent of George's wife or children, was both to ease the King's suffering and to ensure that the King's death be announced in the morning edition of The Times, rather than the "less appropriate" evening editions.

Moments after her husband's death, Queen Mary knelt down and kissed her eldest son's hand, paying homage to the new sovereign in the traditional way. Immediately, the Prince signaled his intention to break away from traditional values by setting the clocks at Sandringham, always half an hour ahead to maximize hunting time, to Greenwich Mean Time and took on the name Edward in solidarity with his grandfather, Edward VII. Prince Albert took the death of his father very hard and mourned the loss not only of the old King but of the familiar and happy family life he had presided over. The court of King Edward VIII soon rose up out of the ashes of the court of George V, one that glittered with all the smartest and most fashionable people of London society. Relations between Prince Albert and King Edward became strained as Albert found himself sidelined in important matters of family and state.

Edward VIII isolated and offended key figures in court, government, and church with his ignorance of his constitutional powers and impatience for tradition. Edward's personal feeling was that it was time to concede India's Dominion status and "realize Indian aspirations," a controversial policy towards Empire that he openly discussed without the advice of ministers. Edward was also pro-divorce and, most controversially, was pro-Germany and was willing to go to great lengths to create friendly Anglo-German relations.

The relationship between Wallis and King Edward became even more serious and contentious when, in October 1936, Wallis was granted a divorce from her husband Ernest Wallis on the grounds of his adultery. Now there was no official deterrent, as laid out by law or in the constitution, stopping the King from marrying a twice-divorced American woman, whom the royal family saw as nothing more than an adventuress. Albert tried in vain to make contact with his brother and talk over the increasingly fraught situation in the succeeding months, but Edward refused to talk and refused even to entertain the idea of giving Wallis up.

Edward confronted his Prime Minister, Baldwin, and set out an ultimatum; either the government approved his marriage to Wallis or not, and if not he would abdicate. Contrary to popular belief, Wallis was not urging Edward on during the abdication crisis; in fact, she made it clear that she did not want him to abdicate and sent him letters begging him to reconsider. However, the King had made up his mind. On the 11th of December 1936, Edward officially abdicated the throne of the United Kingdom and Dominions and the title of Emperor of India.

For Albert, this turn of events was shocking and saddening, and he made no attempt to hide his reluctance to be named King. After a meeting with Edward on the 10th of December when it became clear that his nightmare of becoming King was to be realized and under such unfortunate circumstances, Albert went to his mother Queen Mary and there, he wrote in his diary, he "sobbed like a child." As there was no precedent for a voluntary abdication of the throne in British history, it was unclear what sort of financial and legal settlement Edward should expect; the brothers spent days with lawyers figuring out how to divide the royal fortune. The royal palaces Balmoral and Sandringham belonged to Edward as private properties bequeathed to him in George V's will, and so Albert was forced to buy them from him. On Friday 11th of December 1936, Prince Albert, Duke of York succeeded King Edward VIII to become King George VI of Great Britain, Ireland and the Dominions.

Chapter Six

Becoming King George VI

"To give up all that, for this."

—Queen Mary, the Queen Mother, on King Edward VIII

In George VI's first speech as King, given in front of his Accession Council he said, "I meet you today in circumstances which are without parallel in the history of our Country. Now that the duties of Sovereignty have fallen upon Me I declare to you My adherence to the strict principles of constitutional government and My resolve to work before all else for the welfare of the British Commonwealth of Nations. With my wife and helpmeet by My side, I take up the heavy task which lies before Me…"

This speech was part of the new King's solemn promise to his people to make amends for the scandal and upheaval his brother had caused and to perform his duties as monarch in the same serious and dedicated way that his father had. At first, the British public was divided in its opinion of George's suitability to be King. It was clear that George lacked the easy charisma and crowd-pleasing qualities that Edward had embodied, but George was a man of integrity and determination and had a deep understanding of the workings of British industry, unionism, and trade. George's close relationship with his father ensured that he knew far more than Edward ever did about the actual workings of kingship, and his happy home life projected the simple family values the public grew to appreciate.

George's first act as King was to create Edward the Duke of Windsor, denying him the title of "Prince Edward" but allowing him to retain the title HRH. Edward accepted this title amicably, but when it came to the issue of awarding a title to his soon-to-be wife Wallis and agreeing to a suitable annual allowance, the relationship between the brothers took a drastic turn for the worse. Within a year, George and Edward were no longer on speaking terms.

George VI's coronation took place on the 12th of May 1937 at Westminster Abbey. George's first public speech as King took on extreme significance as a clear indicator of his capacity to rule, but when the time came, George performed magnificently, delivering his speech in a "warm and strong" voice that was recorded by the BBC and replayed in the homes of millions of subjects. George's wife Elizabeth was invested with the ancient Order of the Garter and officially became Queen Consort.

On the day of Edward VIII's abdication, the parliament of the Irish Free State, the Oireachtas, made an amendment to the Irish Constitution that removed all mention of the monarch in a bid to create an Irish republic that retained its links to the Commonwealth. However, Ireland's rejection of the monarchy was not the most distressing matter George had to deal with in his early days as King. Between the end of 1936 and the summer on 1937, while the British government was focused on the unfolding internal drama of Edward's abdication, the political situation in Europe was becoming increasingly tense while Prime Minister Neville

Chamberlain went to great lengths to appease Hitler in Germany and Mussolini in Italy by coming to an amicable settlement that would retract the more objectionable terms of the Treaty of Versailles.

Despite Chamberlain's efforts to come to a rational and fair agreement with Europe's two most tyrannical dictators, Britain found herself inching closer and closer towards a repeat performance of the devastating Great War. On the 12th of March 1938, Germany annexed Austria. As Hitler made his intention to invade Czechoslovakia next obvious, the King and Queen made their first state visit to France, sending a clear message that Great Britain and France were strong allies. Chamberlain continued diplomatic efforts with Hitler, trying desperately to come to a peaceful solution while maintaining Britain's position as a protector of allies.

On the 30th of September 1938, Chamberlain signed his name to the Munich Agreement, a settlement that permitted Nazi Germany's annexation of portions of Czechoslovakia with the new territorial designation Sudetenland. The agreement was signed by Germany, France, the United Kingdom, and Italy, and seemed at first like a promise of peace. George was ecstatic with Chamberlain's efforts, and the British people sighed in relief that war had been averted. However, sacrificing Czechoslovakia to Hitler did not avert war but merely slowed it down. After Hitler's army had marched into the Sudetenland the area ceded more territory to Poland and Yugoslavia and Winston Churchill, then a Conservative MP in the House of Commons, made a damning speech against what he referred to as "the abandonment and ruin of Czechoslovakia."

Churchill's warning that Hitler's increasing power might give him the boldness to one day "look westward" was soon to come true, and Great Britain tried frantically to prepare itself for imminent war. In May 1939, with all of Europe on tenterhooks for the outbreak of war, the King and Queen made an important state tour of Canada and the United States. The Royal couple set sail on the 5th of May 1939 from Southampton aboard the Empress of Australia and on arrival in Ottawa were joined by Canadian Prime Minister William Lyon Mackenzie King, who accompanied them throughout their tour. George VI became the first reigning British sovereign to visit the former colonies since George III when he entered the United States on the 8th of June 1939. The King and Queen disembarked from a train at Washington Union Station and were greeted by President Roosevelt and the First Lady, Mrs. Roosevelt.

The King and Queen's tour of the United States was fraught with the potential for political failure. At the time North America was divided in its opinion of Great Britain, and isolationist factions could be found in many major cities, particularly New York where many of the Irish, Italian, Jewish, and West Indian population had little warm feeling for the British. In general, the American public was also pro-Duke of Windsor and supported Edward VIII's decision to marry Wallis Simpson, an American citizen, without giving up his throne. Yet the tour was a great success, the King and Queen were jubilantly received by the public, and they managed to strike up a strong bond with Prime Minister Mackenzie King and President

Roosevelt that would prove instrumental in bringing the imminent Second World War to an end.

Chapter Seven

The Second World War

"The decisive struggle is now upon us…it is no mere territorial conquest that our enemies are seeking. It is the overthrow, complete and final, of this Empire and of everything for which it stands, and after that the conquest of the world."

—King George VI

On the 3rd of September 1939, Great Britain and the Dominions declared war on Nazi Germany. It was just three months since King George VI and Queen Elizabeth had returned to London from their tour of North America. The King, now sporting the title Head of State and Commander in Chief of the Armed Forces of Great Britain and the Empire, addressed the nation at 6pm in a clear and calm message during which he appealed to his subjects at home and abroad to "stand calm and firm and united" in an unavoidable war that was not of Britain's making.

The King's title was that of a warrior, but his early role in the Second World War was primarily symbolic. With the encouragement of his Prime Minister, Chamberlain, the King did manage to stay remarkably well-informed about the progress of the war; thanks to his naval and air force experience, was able to understand and analyze secret code-breaking intel. In April 1940, the German Army occupied Denmark and attacked Norway. Allied efforts to protect Norway ultimately failed, and on the 10th of May Germany's ground and air forces invaded Holland, Belgium, and Luxembourg in a devastating strategic move that gave Hitler an offensive frontline from the North Sea to the Moselle. Unable to cope with the demands of being Prime Minister during wartime and, unbeknownst to anyone, already ill with stomach cancer, Chamberlain resigned. Winston Churchill took his place as Prime Minister of Great Britain.

George and Elizabeth were determined to stay in London throughout the war and officially lived in Buckingham Palace. In early May 1940, George and Elizabeth were already playing host to a royal refugee, King Haakon of Norway, when Queen Wilhemina of the Netherlands contacted George directly, begging for British military aid. The Queen was brought to England against her will aboard British Destroyer HMS Hereward on the 13th of May and remained a refugee in the United Kingdom throughout the war, later making trips to America and Canada. On the 15th of May, the Dutch army surrendered. Next, Germany invaded France, and on the 14th of June entered the city of Paris with no military objection.

Now the British Empire was the only European power left to fight the Nazi army and war reached the home front. Hitler attacked Great Britain directly for the first time on the 7th of September 1940, a date that later became known as the first night of the Blitz. From the earliest days of the Blitz, the King, the Queen, and their two daughters spent their days working for the war effort in London and their nights at Windsor. A number of ministers expressed their concern at the danger the royal family were exposing themselves to and suggested that the princesses at least be sent to live in Canada for safety. The King and Queen furiously disagreed and, on the 13th of September 1940, narrowly escaped death when German bombs exploded in the courtyard at Buckingham Palace, yards from where they stood.

The King and Queen practiced shooting on the grounds at Windsor, and the young royal couple - photographed visiting bomb sites, rousing troops, sharing the same dangers and enduring the same rations and deprivations as the rest of the nation - became powerful symbols of British pride and united national resistance. Visits to the East End of London, in particular, where over 1000 civilians were killed between the 7th and 8th of September 1940, served to forge a deep bond of respect between the King and his people.

From the beginning of the Blitz, King George and Churchill met privately every Tuesday lunchtime for four years to discuss the war effort in complete secrecy. These meetings were instructive in creating an incredibly close personal relationship between Churchill and the King that would endure even after the war had come to an end. In the Battle of the Atlantic that lasted throughout spring and summer 1941, German U-boats successfully blocked convoys from America making it to Great Britain, and the King hoped and prayed that, should President Roosevelt be re-elected, he would bring America into the war and, by defeating the Germans in the Atlantic, end the war altogether.

Eventually, King George wrote a long personal letter to President Roosevelt to which he received no reply. America's hopes of staying out of the war came crashing to an abrupt end when, on the morning of Sunday 7th December 1941, the Japanese attacked the US Pacific Fleet at Pearl Harbour. The United States and Great Britain jointly declared war on Japan, prompting the other two major axis powers, Italy and Germany, to declare war on the United States.

As 1942 rolled on, news from the allied battlefronts grew more and more distressing, culminating in the surrender of 85,000 British soldiers in Singapore, an event Churchill later described as "the greatest military disaster in recent history." Soon after, in August 1942, the King's brother Prince George, Duke of Kent, was killed in an accident while on active service. A passenger on a Sunderland flying boat, the Duke was on his way to inspect RAF installations in Iceland when the aircraft, flying too low over a hilly region of Scotland in foggy weather, crashed into the top of a hill and exploded in a fireball on the moorland below. Deeply distressed, the King attended his brother's funeral at St George's Chapel at Windsor; just two weeks later, he made an emotional pilgrimage to the site of the crash.

Allied forces landed in North Africa in November 1942, and the King became anxious about an American deal to bring Vichy French forces into the area, further complicating the tense relationship between the heads of occupied and unoccupied France. In June 1943, the King himself visited military forces in North Africa where he was greeted by Dwight D. Eisenhower, Supreme

Commander of the Allied Expeditionary Forces in Europe. The King hosted a tense lunch during which he sat between the two rival French Generals, Giraud and de Gaulle, but succeeded in speaking good French to both and making the lunch a "great success." Next, the King visited American troops at a training camp in Oran before moving on to visit the English army in Tripoli. When the King returned from Algiers on the 25th of June he was exhausted, sunburnt and a stone lighter in weight.

Finally, Allied forces returned to the European mainland and orchestrated the famous Normandy landings on D-Day, 6th of June 1944. One week later King George left London and began a dangerous trip to visit the beaches at Normandy just as Hitler launched his devastating new weapon, the VI flying bomb. The King went on to tour the Italian front between the 23rd of July and 3rd of August before flying to Naples. The Battle of Normandy reached its climax at the end of August 1944, a victory for the Allies that seemed to signal that a triumphant end to the war was within sight.

Invigorated by these few weeks spent living the life of a soldier, albeit a soldier kept out of harm's way, and free of his dreary lifestyle at Windsor, the King intended to continue his tour with a trip to India in February 1945. The King's plans came to nothing as Churchill would not allow a visit, and the Indian Empire soon entered the first stages of dissolution without King George ever setting foot there. Across the Atlantic, on the 12th of April 1945, Franklin D. Roosevelt died suddenly at his cottage in Warm Spring, Georgia, too soon to see victory in the Second World War.

On the 26th of April, the Allied army crossed the River Rhine and, in military terms at least, brought the Second World War to an end. Four days later Hitler committed suicide in his bunker in Berlin, and on the 7th of May 1945, the German High Command agreed to an unconditional surrender to the Western Allies. The official announcement of the end of the war in Great Britain was made at 3pm on the 8th of May by Winston Churchill. During VE day, celebrations in London crowds gathered outside Buckingham Palace shouting "we want the King!" King George invited Churchill out onto the balcony with the royal family to whom the crowds reacted with rapturous applause.

Chapter Eight

Post-War Years

"I declare before you all that my whole life, whether it be long or short, shall be devoted to your service."

—Princess Elizabeth, later Queen Elizabeth II

The summer following the end of the Second World War was a time of celebration and hardship. In Europe, the discovery of the Nazi's concentration camps revealed the true horror of Hitler's final solution and the persecution of Eastern Europeans who had survived occupation led to mass executions. King George knew that his work in Europe was far from over and that to broker an agreement with the Russians at Yalta was one thing but to force them to stand by their promises was quite another. At home, men returned from the war to find their homes in ruin and with few ways to earn a living; homelessness and poverty reached new levels. The treasury was devastated, and the government had few resources to support its starving citizens.

In July 1945, a general election was called and resulted in a crushing defeat for the Conservative Party and a landslide victory for Labour. The Conservatives lost 160 seats while Labour gained 230, giving them a massive advantage in the House of Commons. On the 26th of July Churchill was forced to drive to Buckingham Palace and hand over his letter of resignation to the King, who was moved by the loss of his closest colleague and friend. Clement Atlee became the next Prime Minister of Great Britain, but the King found it difficult to stop going to Churchill for counsel, and he continued to pass on official documents and letters for his opinion.

King George also took it as his personal responsibility to protect the lives of his fellow monarchs in Europe, some of whom he was directly related to. With Churchill's support, the King managed to save Greece from the threat of communist guerrillas, restoring Greek democracy and placing the King of Greece, who had spent the war as a refugee in London, back on his throne. Great Britain refused, however, to intervene when Russia installed a puppet communist government in Romania.

In America, Harry Truman became the next President of the United States, and the King met with him on the 2nd of August 1945 to discuss Russian power and America's recent secret testing of the atomic bomb. A few days after this meeting, on the 6th of August 1945, the first a-bomb was dropped on Hiroshima. On the 9th of August, a second a-bomb was dropped on Nagasaki, and Japan offered its unconditional surrender on the 15th of August 1945.

For six of the ten years of King George's reign, Great Britain had been at war. Now, King George had to adjust to the post-war period with a strong Labour government primed to revolutionize life in Great Britain with a series of radical social changes. The King was known to be incredibly well-informed on the inner workings of the government and spent a great deal of time familiarizing himself with official papers in order to challenge ministers whenever he could. The strong democratic spirit of the post-war years threatened King George's authority and the monarchy as a whole, and the threat of serious social revolution hung over the country. Matters were made worse in 1947 when Britain experienced one of the worst winters on record and a major fuel crisis led in turn to huge unemployment and devastating financial collapse. The King was forced to announce a suspension of the convertibility of the pound, and it became clear that Britain could no longer afford her empire.

Certain dominions of the British Empire had already evolved into separate sovereign states due to the Statute of Westminster 1931. The British Empire was already in the early stages of its dissolution in the 1930s, but the advent of the Second World War in 1939 greatly sped up this process. The King mourned the loss of Singapore, Hong Kong, and Malaya, independent states that now acknowledged their association with Great Britain through membership of the Commonwealth. In 1947 the British Indian Empire split in two, becoming the Dominion of Pakistan and the Union of India. The partition of India and the subsequent religious genocide it inspired led to the largest mass migration of people in history, with an estimated 2,000,000 Muslim and Hindu people killed.

As a sovereign democratic republic, India refused to acknowledge King George as King of India but remained in the Commonwealth. It was agreed that allegiance to the Crown would no longer be necessary to retain membership to the Commonwealth and the British Crown was transformed from a symbol of domination to a symbol of association. Burma left the Commonwealth in 1948,

Palestine left in May 1948, and the Republic of Ireland on Easter Monday, 1949.

In February 1947, with Britain still suffering the hardships of a major fuel crisis, the royal family boarded the battleship *HMS Vanguard* and embarked on a tour of South Africa. The King's friend Field Marshal Jan Smuts was facing an election to retain his status as Prime Minister against the Nationalist Party. The King was reluctant to leave his country in a time of need, but canceling the tour would only magnify the crisis in the eyes of the world. During the tour, which involved a three-week voyage followed by two months spent almost constantly on a train, the King's health was under strain, and he became aggravated on a number of occasions with his South African bodyguards, whom he nicknamed "the Gestapo." The King still felt that, despite the passing of the Indian Empire, the United Kingdom of Great Britain had a role to play beyond its coastlines and turned his full attention to South Africa, a fertile land rich in unmined minerals.

Princess Elizabeth, who turned 21 during the tour of South Africa, made a broadcast speech in April 1947 in which she said, "I should like to make that dedication now. It is very simple. I declare before you all that my whole life, whether it be long or short, shall be devoted to your service and the service of our great Imperial Commonwealth to which we all belong..."

Chapter Nine

Final Years

"The highest of distinctions is service to others."

—King George VI

Back at Sandringham, as the 1940s tentatively approached the 1950s, George's health began to worsen, and his patience for the ceremonious and social side of kingship thinned. Many anecdotes from staff or acquaintances of the King's at this time make much of his frequent fits of temper and expletive-laden rants, but on the whole, the King was considered polite and welcoming. During these years George indulged himself deeply one of his life-long passions, shooting, inviting groups of similarly marksmanship-obsessed friends to Sandringham or Balmoral to practice his favorite sport.

The King's relationship with his family was central to his happiness, and he always fought hard to maintain a closeness and warmth in his home life, despite the demands of public life. As the King's health deteriorated in the late 1940s, he began to encourage Princess Elizabeth, who would undoubtedly succeed him to the throne, to take on his royal duties. Despite turning 18 on the 26th of April 1944, Elizabeth was often referred to as young for her age. In an attempt to ensure that Princess Margaret, the youngest of the pair, did not feel the same inferiority that he did growing up as the younger sibling of an heir to the throne, the King treated the two girls exactly the same. The four-year age gap between the sisters was disregarded and the pair dressed the same, kept the same hours and were exposed to the same company even when Elizabeth reached the age of 18.

King George did not want to see the break-up of his perfect family, but by the time Elizabeth turned 18 he was well aware that she was in love with her cousin, Prince Philip of Greece. A lieutenant in the Royal Navy with a wonderful record and royal blood flowing through his veins, Philip was a perfect match for the young princess. At first, the royal couple was not thrilled with the prospect of having Philip as their son in law, but over time he won them over with his wit and charm. Late in the summer of 1946, the King agreed to Elizabeth and Philip's engagement on the condition that they waited until the South Africa tour was over and Elizabeth's twenty-first birthday had passed.

The engagement of Princess Elizabeth and Prince Philip of Greece was announced to the public in July 1947 and took place on the 20th of November the same year. Britain was in the depths of the harsh austerity of the post-war years and, at the beginning of a bitter winter and subsequent fuel crisis, the royal wedding provided a ray of sunshine during an otherwise drab time. Elizabeth's dress was magnificent, the food was simple, and, thankfully, the speeches were short; after the wedding, the couple escaped to Broadlands House in Hampshire where they spent their honeymoon.

Animosity between King George and his brother the Duke of Windsor only grew in intensity as both men aged.

The King's continued refusal to give the Duchess of Windsor the title of Her Royal Highness and his refusal to receive her spurred the Duke on to involvement with movements that proved to be fronts for the Nazi Party, hoping to regain power in Europe. The Duke was also obsessed with money and was constantly pressuring the King to fund his and Wallis's lavish lifestyle.

The King had been a heavy smoker through his entire life; as he reached his early fifties, he was diagnosed with lung cancer and arteriosclerosis of the heart. Suffering from restricted blood flow to his legs and feet, a direct result of smoking, the King's right foot became dangerously starved of blood, to the point where gangrene had almost set in by the time he sought medical advice. The King's planned tour of New Zealand and Australia was canceled, and he was ordered to rest in bed. On the 14th of November 1948, Elizabeth gave birth to Prince Charles, and only after her son had been safely delivered was she told of the seriousness of her father's condition. On the 12th of March 1949, the King had a lumbar sympathectomy at a special operating theater set up at Buckingham Palace.

Once recovered from the birth of her first child, Elizabeth took on more royal duties and took the place of the King on the delayed royal tour of Australia and New Zealand. On the 23rd of September 1951, the King was forced to go under the surgeon's knife yet again, this time to have his left lung removed. While the King convalesced, a General Election was held. On the 25th of October, the Conservative Party returned to power, led by the King's old brother in arms, Winston Churchill. In the meantime, Princess Elizabeth and Prince Philip had embarked on a hugely successful tour of the United States and Canada, during which they stayed with the Trumans at the White House.

The King was unaware that the operation to remove his lung had not completely eradicated cancer from his body and tried in vain to get back to full strength. In early February 1952, after traveling to the airport to say goodbye to Princess Elizabeth, who was again touring Australia, this time via Kenya, the King returned to his favorite place, Sandringham. The King spent a few days shooting and dining with his wife and daughter; then, on the 6th of February, he died in his sleep from a blood clot in his heart. Princess Elizabeth became Queen Elizabeth II of the United Kingdom of Great Britain while watching Rhino at a game reserve in Kenya.

Conclusion

Public mourning at the death of George VI was deep and far-reaching. When the news broke in London, people stopped what they were doing and even stepped out of their cars to stand to attention and acknowledge the passing of a great King. In America too, where anti-monarchy sentiment was strong even during the post-war years, King George's death was respectfully acknowledged, and formal tribute was made to his dedication to his subjects. President Truman remarked in his private diary, later made public, that King George VI was "worth a pair of his brother Ed."

King George VI never did make peace with his brother, David, Duke of Windsor, formerly King Edward VIII. The brothers had been close and the series of events that led to their estrangement, beginning with Edward's affair with Wallis Simpson, left Albert astounded and horrified but unable to turn back the clock. Edward's abdication and the subsequent burden on kingship that landed squarely on Albert's shoulders could have broken his will, but instead, the unfortunate circumstances of his accession served to make him a stronger and more resilient King. As the King remarked in a letter to his brother directly following the abdication crisis, he had assumed "rocking throne" but would do what he could "to make it steady again."

The throne that George VI ascended to, aged 41, was unsteady in that public opinion of the monarchy was at its worst. Edward VIII's behavior while King and his abdication added fuel to the fire of republicanism that was sweeping the nation. Factions of Parliament began to question the need for the monarchy and the cost to the nation, and while all eyes were watching the royal scandal unfold, political tension in Europe reached crisis point.

That George VI managed to win back public faith even as the devastation of the Second World War rained down on their heads is a testament to his success as King. Honor-bound to fulfill his duty as King through the hard times and the good, George VI remained in London throughout the Blitz and played a key role in the work of the war office throughout the war. In the post-war years, as Britain and her allies realized that victory alone could not rebuild a nation, the King continued to lead and supported important legislative changes to help the worst off in society. The world that King George VI left behind was unrecognizable from the one he knew when he took on the kingship of Great Britain. The effects of a catastrophic world war, the collapse of the British Empire, and the establishment of a socialist government in Great Britain may seem like events that would spell the end of the British monarchy, yet through his resolute sense of duty, impeccable diplomacy, and personal courage, King George VI ensured that the British people would remember him not just as a King, but as a truly great King.

Printed in Great Britain
by Amazon

53157698R00031